Easy Peasy Online Money Making Tools: A Beginners Guide to Get Rich and Retire Early Using Spare Time

I0476149

Why you need this book?

THIS IS THE ONLY BOOK THAT PROVIDES INFORMATION ABOUT EASY PEASY ONLINE MONEY MAKING TOOLS THAT OFFER HIGH PROBABILITY OF SUCCESS.

Now more than ever before, Internet and Mobile phone technology has enabled people to make money in flexible ways. Technology has connected people with businesses throughout the world.

As a result there are many ways you can make money with no stress, no investment, no experience, and no skills. Information Technology (IT) is rapidly changing so we need to make sure we have current information. This book contains only valid and active information about such opportunities.

You need this book if:

You want to earn money online every day
You want to live healthy, wealthy and wise
You want to be your own boss
You want to work from home
You want to Make Money in Your Spare Time
You want to enjoy your life
You want to retire early

You want to pursue your dreams of financial freedom

You want to make money online in your spare-time

You want to solve your money problems forever

You are looking for flexible easy work

You want to Take Charge of Your Finances

You want to retire early

Good Luck,

Robert J Davis

Online Method # 9 to make Extra Cash now in your spare-time with no investment, no experience, and no skills

Make Money in Your Spare Time by Online Money Tool:

Online Method # 10 to make Extra Cash now in your spare-time with no investment, no experience, and no skills

Make Money in Your Spare Time by Online Money Tool:

Online Method # 11 to make Extra Cash now in your spare-time with no investment, no experience, and no skills

Make Money in Your Spare Time by Online Money Tool:

Online Method # 12 to make Extra Cash now in your spare-time with no investment, no experience, and no skills

Make Money in Your Spare Time by Online Money Tool:

Online Method # 13 to make Extra Cash now in your spare-time with no investment, no experience, and no skills

Make Money in Your Spare Time by Online Money Tool:

Online Method # 14 to make Extra Cash now in your spare-time with no investment, no experience, and no skills

Online Method # 15 to make Extra Cash now in your spare-time with no investment, no experience, and no skills

Online Method # 16 to make Extra Cash now in your spare-time with no investment, no experience, and no skills

Online Method # 17 to make Extra Cash now in your spare-time with no investment, no experience, and no skills

Online Method # 18 to make Extra Cash now in your spare-time with no investment, no experience, and no skills

Online Method # 19 to make Extra Cash now in your spare-time with no investment, no experience, and no skills

Make Money in Your Spare Time by Online Money Tool:

Online Method # 20 to make Extra Cash now in your spare-time with no investment, no experience, and no skills

Make Money in Your Spare Time by Online Money Tool:

Online Method # 21 to make Extra Cash now in your spare-time with no investment, no experience, and no skills

Make Money in Your Spare Time by Online Money Tool:

Online Method # 22 to make Extra Cash now in your spare-time with no investment, no experience, and no skills

Make Money in Your Spare Time by Online Money Tool:

Online Method # 23 to make Extra Cash now in your spare-time with no investment, no experience, and no skills

Make Money in Your Spare Time by Online Money Tool:

Online Method # 24 to make Extra Cash now in your spare-time with no investment, no experience, and no skills

Make Money in Your Spare Time by Online Money Tool:

Online Method # 25 to make Extra Cash now in your spare-time with no investment, no experience, and no skills

Make Money in Your Spare Time by Online Money Tool:

Online Method # 26 to make Extra Cash now in your spare-time with no investment, no experience, and no skills

Make Money in Your Spare Time by Online Money Tool:

Online Method #27 to make Extra Cash now in your spare-time with no investment, no experience, and no skills

Make Money in Your Spare Time by Online Money Tool:

Online Method #28 to make Extra Cash now in your spare-time with no investment, no experience, and no skills

Make Money in Your Spare Time by Online Money Tool:

Online Method # 29 to make Extra Cash now in your spare-time with no investment, no experience, and no skills

Make Money in Your Spare Time by Online Money Tool:

Online Method # 30 to make Extra Cash now in your spare-time with no investment, no experience, and no skills

Make Money in Your Spare Time by Online Money Tool:

Online Method #31 to make Extra Cash now in your spare-time with no investment, no experience, and no skills

Make Money in Your Spare Time by Online Money Tool:

Online Method #32 to make Extra Cash now in your spare-time with no investment, no experience, and no skills

Make Money in Your Spare Time by Online Money Tool:

Online Method # 33 to make Extra Cash now in your spare-time with no investment, no experience, and no skills

Make Money in Your Spare Time by Online Money Tool:

Online Method #34 to make Extra Cash now in your spare-time with no investment, no experience, and no skills

Make Money in Your Spare Time by Online Money Tool:

Online Method #35 to make Extra Cash now in your spare-time with no investment, no experience, and no skills

Make Money in Your Spare Time by Online Money Tool:

Online Method # to make Extra Cash now in your spare-time with no investment, no experience, and no skills

Make Money in Your Spare Time by Online Money Tool:

Online Method #36 to make Extra Cash now in your spare-time with no investment, no experience, and no skills

Make Money in Your Spare Time by Online Money Tool:

Online Method #37 to make Extra Cash now in your spare-time with no investment, no experience, and no skills

Online Method #38 to make Extra Cash now in your spare-time with no investment, no experience, and no skills

Online Method #39 to make Extra Cash now in your spare-time with no investment, no experience, and no skills

Online Method #40 to make Extra Cash now in your spare-time with no investment, no experience, and no skills

Generate Residual income now for Retiring Young

What to do with Extra Cash?

Become a Millionaire and Retire Young. Also to take care of all these expenses for living the Good Life:

- ❖ Books

- ❖ Cable Television

- ❖ Car Repairs

- ❖ Clothing

- ❖ Electricity

- ❖ Entertainment

- ❖ Gas

- ❖ Groceries

- ❖ Home Maintenance

- ❖ Household Furnishings

- ❖ Insurance

- ❖ Internet

- ❖ Laundry

- ❖ Leased Equipment

- ❖ Magazines

- ❖ Meals Out

- ❖ Medical Expenses

- ❖ Mortgage

- ❖ Oil

- ❖ Personal Care

- ❖ Pets

- ❖ Property Taxes

- ❖ Rent

- ❖ Storage

- ❖ Transportation

- ❖ Travel

- ❖ Vacations

So let's start making some extra cash now!

Everyone has potential to make millions online by using the tools mentioned in this book.

Because its very simple and do not require any higher education or professional qualifications its perfect for anyone including housewives where they can easily earn extra cash in free time by working from anywhere.

The problem we all have is that we start wasting money in useless things and we land up in debt.

I would like you to make the most of your extra money you earn by any of these tools.

Let us say you are in your 20's and you started making $100 extra cash a day using the tools in this book.

If you make extra cash $100 daily, you will have $3000 extra cash monthly.

To reap the most benefit from your extra money, you need to start saving now.

Let us say you can only save half of it so its $50 a day.

That's $1500 a month.

You should put that money in compound interest investments and you'll be able to create your millions for your future as calculated below:

Compound Interest Calculation when you invest equal amounts of money once a month:

Multiple Investments in Equal Amounts every month:

Payment	x		=	Amount Investment is Worth
		$(1+\text{Interest Rate})\text{Time Period}-1$		
		Interest Rate		

Current Principal: $ 1500

Monthly Addition: $ 1500

Years to Grow: 25

Interest Rate: 7 %

Compound Interest time(s) per year: 2

Future Value $1,187,358.58

As you can see you will have one million, one hundred eighty-seven thousand, three hundred fifty-eight and fifty-eight hundredths dollars by the time you are in your *FORTIES.*

Online Method # 1 to make Extra Cash now in your spare-time with no investment, no experience, and no skills

Make Money in Your Spare Time by Online Money Tool:

Amazon Mechanical Turk

Amazon Mechanical Turk
https://www.mturk.com/

How can I earn money online by Mturk?
Mturk will pay you for:

    I.   **Submitting polls**
    II.   **Completing special offers**
    III.   **Shopping**
    IV.   **Playing Games**
    V.   **Using the Search function**
    VI.   **Submitting highway photos**
    VII.   **Classifying Web sites**

Online Method # 2 to make Extra Cash now in your spare-time with no investment, no experience, and no skills

Make Money in Your Spare Time by Online Money Tool:

ClixSense

ClixSense: Make Money Taking Surveys
www.clixsense.com/

How Can I Make Money on Clixsense?

You can earn money for:

     I.   **Taking up surveys online**
    II.   **Submitting reports**
   III.   **For Visiting Ads**
   IV.   **Visiting Websites And**
    V.   **Referring Others**
   VI.   **Completing Survey**
  VII.   **Completing Task**
 VIII.   **For Referral**

Online Method # 3 to make Extra Cash now in your spare-time with no investment, no experience, and no skills

Make Money in Your Spare Time by Online Money Tool:

Fiverr

Fiverr: The marketplace for creative & professional services
https://www.fiverr.com/

How Can I Make Money on Fiverr?

You can earn money when you complete tasks:

    I.   **Translation**
   II.   **Writing**

III. Video
IV. Music
 V. Audio Production
VI. Social Marketing
VII. Graphics

Online Method # 4 to make Extra Cash now in your spare-time with no investment, no experience, and no skills

Make Money in Your Spare Time by Online Money Tool:

GigBull

gigbull - Gigbucks
https://gigbucks.com/user/gigbull

How Can I Make Money on gigbull?

You can earn money when you:

I.   **Complete Micro Job**
II.   **Complete Online Tasks**
III.   **Writing**
IV.   **Translation**
V.   **Video**
VI.   **Music**
VII.   **Audio Production**

Online Method # 5 to make Extra Cash now in your spare-time with no investment, no experience, and no skills

Make Money in Your Spare Time by Online Money Tool:

Microworkers

Microworkers - work & earn or offer a micro job
https://microworkers.com/

How Can I Make Money on Microworkers?

You can earn money when you:

     I.   Review a Google app
     II.   Participate in free trials
     III.   Search on Face book
     IV.   Watch You Tube video and like it
     V.   Watch a video and leave a comment
     VI.   Bookmark pages of other sites
     VII.   Tweet to promote something
     VIII.   Rate videos or articles
     IX.   Vote for contest entries
     X.   Blog

Online Method # 6 to make Extra Cash now in your spare-time with no investment, no experience, and no skills

Make Money in Your Spare Time by Online Money Tool: userfeel.com

UserFeel.com: Remote Usability Testing
www.userfeel.com/

You can earn money by providing services:

I.   **Website Tester**
II.   **Usability Test**
III.   **User Testing**
IV.   **Type Of Micro Job: Website Tester**
V.   **Giving Feedback**

Online Method # 7 to make Extra Cash now in your spare-time with no investment, no experience, and no skills

Make Money in Your Spare Time by Online Money Tool: Youtube

 https://www.youtube.com

You can earn money by using these steps:

I.   **Sign up for your YouTube account**
II.   **Create your YouTube Channel**
III.   **Enable your channel for monetization.**
IV.   **Make Video**
V.   **Upload Video**
VI.   **Set up AdSense**
VII. **Enable Monetization to Start Earning**
VIII. **Connect your YouTube channel to an AdSense**

Online Method # 8 to make Extra Cash now in your spare-time with no investment, no experience, and no skills

Make Money in Your Spare Time by Online Money Tool:

Appen (Appen Butler Hill)

Appen
www.appen.com/

How Can I Make Money on Appen?

You can earn money for completing crowd sourcing short tasks

Online Method # 9 to make Extra Cash now in your spare-time with no investment, no experience, and no skills

Make Money in Your Spare Time by Online Money Tool:

Coin Worker

CoinWorker - get bitcoin over the web
https://coinworker.com/

How Can I Make Money on Coin worker?

You can earn money for:

I. **Taking up surveys online**
II. **Submitting reports**

Online Method # 10 to make Extra Cash now in your spare-time with no investment, no experience, and no skills

Make Money in Your Spare Time by Online Money Tool:

Embee Mobile

Embee Mobile: Mobile insight panels & technology solutions
embeemobile.com/

How Can I Make Money on Embee Mobile?

You can earn money when you:
I. **Perform tasks for customers**
II. **Participate in surveys**

Online Method # 11 to make Extra Cash now in your spare-time with no investment, no experience, and no skills

Make Money in Your Spare Time by Online Money Tool:

Fittytown

Fittytown

www.fittytown.com/

How Can I Make Money on Fittytown?

You can earn money when you complete tasks:
  I.   **Micro jobs Online**
  II.   **Freelance Jobs**
  III.   **Make Money Online**
  IV.   **Buy Sell Services**
  V.   **Internet Articles**
  VI.   **Internet Videos**

Online Method # 12 to make Extra Cash now in your spare-time with no investment, no experience, and no skills

Make Money in Your Spare Time by Online Money Tool:

Fivesquids

Things people do for a fiver. Everything 5 pounds - fivesquid
https://www.fivesquid.com/

How Can I Make Money on Five squids?

You can earn money when you:

I. **Trade skills**
II. **Trade services**

Online Method # 13 to make Extra Cash now in your spare-time with no investment, no experience, and no skills

Make Money in Your Spare Time by Online Money Tool:

Inbox Dollars

InboxDollars
www.inboxdollars.com/

.
How Can I Make Money on inbox dollars?

You can earn money when you:

I.   Complete Micro Job: Surveys
II.   Participate In Rewards Program
III.   Watch Ads
IV.   Take Surveys
V.   Shop Online
VI.   Redeem Coupons
VII.   Receive Emails
VIII.   Play Games

Online Method # 14 to make Extra Cash now in your spare-time with no investment, no experience, and no skills

Make Money in Your Spare Time by Online Money Tool: DoMyStuff

DoMyStuff.com - Outsource your life
www.domystuff.com/

How Can I Make Money on Domystuff?

I.   Pick up a task posted by people on DoMyStuff
II. Bid on a task
III. If your bid is accepted
IV. Complete the task and you will get paid

Online Method # 15 to make Extra Cash now in your spare-time with no investment, no experience, and no skills

Make Money in Your Spare Time by Online Money Tool: Clickworker

ClickWorker
https://www.clickworker.com/

How can I earn money online by Clickworker?

Clickworker pays you for:

    I.   **Writing**
    II. **Translating**
   III. **researching**
  IV. **data processing**

Online Method # 16 to make Extra Cash now in your spare-time with no investment, no experience, and no skills

Make Money in Your Spare Time by Online Money Tool: Swagbucks

Swagbucks
www.swagbucks.com/

How can I earn money online by Swagbucks?

Swag bucks will pay you for:

VIII. Submitting polls
IX. Completing special offers
X. Shopping
XI. Playing Games
XII. Using the Search function
XIII. Watching SBTV

Online Method # 17 to make Extra Cash now in your spare-time with no investment, no experience, and no skills

Make Money in Your Spare Time by Online Money Tool: Fieldagent

Become an Agent Today | Field Agent
https://fieldagent.net/for-agents/

How can I earn money online by Field Agent?

Field Agent is a smart phone app; it will pay you for:

I. Completing a task using your smart phone
II. You act as the eyes and ears of a company
III. Completing opinion surveys
IV. Completing location-based surveys

Online Method # 18 to make Extra Cash now in your spare-time with no investment, no experience, and no skills

Make Money in Your Spare Time by Online Money Tool: MyLOT

myLot / Make money
www.mylot.com/

How can I earn money online at Mylot?

My Lot will pay you when:
  I.   You post a new discussion
  II. You respond to current discussion
  III. You comment on a current discussion
  IV. You refer someone

Online Method # 19 to make Extra Cash now in your spare-time with no investment, no experience, and no skills

Make Money in Your Spare Time by Online Money Tool:

weeklymarks.com

weeklymarks.com
weeklymarks.com/

How Can I Make Money on weekly marks?

You can earn money when you:

      I.   **Participate in Surveys That Pay**
      II.   **Complete Jobs**
      III.   **Virtual Data Entry**

Online Method # 20 to make Extra Cash now in your spare-time with no investment, no experience, and no skills

Make Money in Your Spare Time by Online Money Tool:

InstantBucks

www.instantbucks.com/

How Can I Make Money on ipinion?

You can earn money when you:

      I.   **Participate in Surveys**
      II.   **Participate in rewards program**

Online Method # 21 to make Extra Cash now in your spare-time with no investment, no experience, and no skills

Make Money in Your Spare Time by Online Money Tool:

Ipinions

iPinion Rewards
secure.ipinionrewards.com/

How Can I Make Money on ipinion?

You can earn money when you:

I.   **Participate in a Surveys on mobile phone**
II.   **Download the free app**

Online Method # 22 to make Extra Cash now in your spare-time with no investment, no experience, and no skills

Make Money in Your Spare Time by Online Money Tool:

Mylikes

MyLikes - maximize your value on social media

mylikes.com/

You can earn money by:

I.   Social media advertising

II.   Content creation

Online Method # 23 to make Extra Cash now in your spare-time with no investment, no experience, and no skills

Make Money in Your Spare Time by Online Money Tool:

QuickTate

Quicktate
www.quicktate.com/

You can earn money by:

I.   **Writing Jobs**
II.   **Data Entry Jobs**
III.   **Transcription Jobs**
IV.   **Transcribe Voicemails,**
V.   **Personal Dictations,**
VI.   **Call Recordings**

Online Method # 24 to make Extra Cash now in your spare-time with no investment, no experience, and no skills

Make Money in Your Spare Time by Online Money Tool:

Redlr

REDLR.COM | Make Money Online | Freelancer | Micro Jobs
blog.redlr.com/

How Can I Make Money on REDLR?

You can earn money when you:

    I.   **Post topics**
   II.   **Post reply to others**
  III.   **Discussions**

Online Method # 25 to make Extra Cash now in your spare-time with no investment, no experience, and no skills

Make Money in Your Spare Time by Online Money Tool:

Scribie

Scribie Audio/Video Transcription
https://scribie.com/

How Can I Make Money on Scribie?

I.   **You are paid per audio hour for what you transcribe**
II.   **Transcription review and proofreading**

Online Method # 26 to make Extra Cash now in your spare-time with no investment, no experience, and no skills

Make Money in Your Spare Time by Online Money Tool:

Shopkick

Shopkick

https://www.shopkick.com/

How Can I Make Money on Shopkick?

You can earn money by:

I.   **Rewards program**
II.   **Online and real-world tasks via mobile phone**
III.   **Earn points when you make purchases**

Online Method #27 to make Extra Cash now in your spare-time with no investment, no experience, and no skills

Make Money in Your Spare Time by Online Money Tool:

Skyword

Skyword: The Art and Science of Content Marketing
www.skyword.com/

How Can I Make Money on Skyword?

You can earn money by completing simple tasks:

I. **Content creation**
II. **Publishing**
III. **Residual income for writing**

Online Method #28 to make Extra Cash now in your spare-time with no investment, no experience, and no skills

Make Money in Your Spare Time by Online Money Tool:

StartUpLift

StartUpLift

startuplift.com/

How Can I Make Money on Startuplift?

You can earn money by completing simple tasks:

I.   **Get Paid To Provide Feedback**
II.   **Startups provide their website URL**

Online Method # 29 to make Extra Cash now in your spare-time with no investment, no experience, and no skills

Make Money in Your Spare Time by Online Money Tool:

TryMYUI

Become a Tester - TryMyUI
www.trymyui.com/worker/signup

How Can I Make Money on TryMYUI?

You can earn money by completing simple tasks:

I.   **Remote website testing**
II.   **Test opportunities via email**
III.   **Provide feedback on website**
IV.   **Remote Usability Testing**

Online Method # 30 to make Extra Cash now in your spare-time with no investment, no experience, and no skills

Make Money in Your Spare Time by Online Money Tool:

Viggle

Viggle:
get.viggle.com/

How Can I Make Money on Viggle?

You can earn money by completing simple tasks:

I.   Make Money By Watching TV using Viggle

II.   By answering trivia questions

III.   Voting in polls

IV.   Using social media

V.   Referring new customers

Online Method #31 to make Extra Cash now in your spare-time with no investment, no experience, and no skills

Make Money in Your Spare Time by Online Money Tool:

Zaarly

Become a Service Expert - Zaarly
www.zaarly.com/businesses

How Can I Make Money on Zaarly?

You can earn money by providing services:

     I.   House Cleaning
     II.   Handyman
     III.   Lawn Care Services...etc

Online Method #32 to make Extra Cash now in your spare-time with no investment, no experience, and no skills

Make Money in Your Spare Time by Online Money Tool:

CashCrate

Make Money Online With Paid Surveys
www.cashcrate.com/

How Can I Make Money on CashCrate?

You can earn money by completing simple tasks:

     I.   Completing offers
     II.   Taking surveys
     III.   Watching videos
     IV.   Completing online tasks
     V.   Shopping online via Cash Crate

Online Method # 33 to make Extra Cash now in your spare-time with no investment, no experience, and no skills

Make Money in Your Spare Time by Online Money Tool:

CrowdFlower

CrowdFlower | Make your data useful
www.crowdflower.com/

How Can I Make Money on Crowd Flower?

You can earn money by completing simple tasks:

I.   **Internet research**
II.   **Data collection**
III. **Data categorization**
IV.   **Content creation**
V.   **Content moderation**
VI.   **Surveys**

Online Method #34 to make Extra Cash now in your spare-time with no investment, no experience, and no skills

Make Money in Your Spare Time by Online Money Tool:

EasyShift

EasyShift
easyshiftapp.com/

How Can I Make Money on Easyshift?

I.   **EasyShift is a mircotask app where you can earn money by completing task on your iPhone**

II.   **Manufacturers and distributors submit tasks on EasyShift**
III.   **These Tasks may ask you to conduct an audit of retail outlets for them**

Online Method #35 to make Extra Cash now in your spare-time with no investment, no experience, and no skills

Make Money in Your Spare Time by Online Money Tool:

FusionCash

FusionCash: Paid Surveys, Videos, Cashback
www.fusioncash.net/

How Can I Make Money on FusionCash?

Online Method # to make Extra Cash now in your spare-time with no investment, no experience, and no skills

Make Money in Your Spare Time by Online Money Tool:

Gig Coin

GigCoin
gigcoin.com/

How Can I Make Money on Gig coin?

I. You are paid for completing small tasks
II. Complete tasks online and via their iPhone app
III. Select for Micro Tasks such as surveys, writing, or promoting a product
IV. Complete the tasks and get paid

Online Method #36 to make Extra Cash now in your spare-time with no investment, no experience, and no skills

Make Money in Your Spare Time by Online Money Tool:

GigWalk

Gigwalk
www.gigwalk.com/

How Can I Make Money on GigWalk?

I. It's a crowd-sourced service
II. You can make money by smart phones by completing short tasks such as taking pictures of Menu
III. Gig Walk uses your smartphone's GPS location info to show you tasks in your area
IV. Visit a wireless store and check on product placement for a cell phone manufacturer
V. Test out a new phone app

Online Method #37 to make Extra Cash now in your spare-time with no investment, no experience, and no skills

Make Money in Your Spare Time by Online Money Tool: TaskRabbit

TaskRabbit
https://www.taskrabbit.com/

How Can I Make Money on Taskrabbit?

I. **Pickup a short task**

II. **Complete that physical tasks such as handyman work etc and you will get paid**

Online Method #38 to make Extra Cash now in your spare-time with no investment, no experience, and no skills

Make Money in Your Spare Time by Online Money Tool: Shutterstock

Shutterstock
www.shutterstock.com/

How Can I Make Money on Shutterstock?

I. **You will need a camera; you make money by by selling your photography to Shutter stock**

II.   Shutter stock has a subscription payment plan where buyers pay a monthly fee

III.

Online Method #39 to make Extra Cash now in your spare-time with no investment, no experience, and no skills

Make Money in Your Spare Time by Online Money Tool: Logoworks

Company - Logoworks | Professional Logo Design, www.logoworks.com/company/

How Can I Make Money on Logoworks?

I.   **Logoworks is an online graphic design company**
II.   **You will be paid for logo design, web design, and other advertising services**

Online Method #40 to make Extra Cash now in your spare-time with no investment, no experience, and no skills

Make Money in Your Spare Time by Online Money Tool: Worldwide 101

Worldwide101 Virtual Assistants for Business worldwide101.com/jobs

How Can I Make Money on Worldwide 101?

It's a virtual assistant company; you will be paid for working as Virtual Assistant or cyber secretary.

Generate Residual income now for Retiring Young

Some of the extra cash should be invested now in the opportunities that pay a monthly dividend (any distribution of cash paid to shareholders)

About the author/editor/compiler:
Robert J Davis has been involved in the education space for the past 10 years.

www.ingramcontent.com/pod-product-compliance
Lightning Source LLC
Chambersburg PA
CBHW071818170526
45167CB00003B/1362